Fairyland Mail

Poems by

Marge Hauser

 NoNet Press, New York City

Fairyland Mail

First North American Publication 2014

Copyright © 2014 Margery Hauser

All rights reserved. Except for use in any review or for educational purposes, the reproduction or utilization of this work in whole or in part is forbidden without the written permission of the publisher or author. NoNet Press, nonetpress@gmail.com. Margery Hauser can be reached by email addressed to mhauser@nyc.rr.com.

Printed in the U.S.A.
Cover Photo: Fairy Tree, by Margery Hauser
Author Photo: by Priscilla Marira

I am eternally grateful to my father, whose mixed-up bedtime stories inspired my love of whimsy; to Marcy Stone for introducing me to Jack B. Nimble, Attorney at Law who facilitated the acquisition of these private missives; and always to my friends and fellow poets of the Parkside Collective, without whose support, feedback and encouragement this collection would not exist.

We gratefully acknowledge the following journals where some of these poems have previously appeared:

Bohemia Art & Literary Journal
    Mary Had a Little Lamb
    Georgie Porgie

First Literary Review-East
    Old Mother Hubbard
    Mary, Mary, Quite Contrary

Ides of March
    Hansel and Gretel

The Literary Lawyer
    Three Little Pigs
    Peter Pumpkineater (Mr. & Mrs. P)
    Rumpelstiltskin
    Three Blind Mice

From: me@author.com
Subject: Table of Contents
To: you@reader.com

Snow White	1
The Three Little Pigs	2
Humpty Dumpty	3
Jack and the Beanstalk (Jack)	4
Jack and the Beanstalk (Giant)	5
Hansel and Gretel	6
Mary Had a Little Lamb	7
Goldilocks and the Three Bears	8
Georgie Porgie	9
Peter, Peter Pumpkineater (Mr. P.)	10
Peter, Peter Pumpkineater (Mrs.P.)	11
Cinderella	12
Old Mother Hubbard	13
Little Boy Blue	14
Mary, Mary Quite Contrary	15
The Pied Piper	16
Little Miss Muffet	17
Rumpelstiltskin	18
Three Blind Mice	19
The Old Woman Who Lived in a Shoe	20
Little Red Riding Hood	21

From: mmirror@chamber.com
Subject: Tempus Fugit
To: hermajesty@castle.net

Of course I understand. You had no choice.
You used to be the fairest of the fair
with unlined skin, bright eyes and long, dark
      hair.
Your beauty was proclaimed by every voice
throughout the land. You were the one adored
by all . . . and then, alas, *she* came of age.
That grubby child grew up. Time turned the
      page
and suddenly it was her star that soared.
You had no choice, I know. I understand.
She had to be removed, but by whose hand?
An apple and a huntsman and a spell –
soon she'd be gone and then all would be well.
But listen close, hear that derisive laughter.
You failed. There is no happily ever after.

From: mgoose@fairylaw.com
Subject: Civil Suit
To: mrsb.b.wolf@lair.com

We've read the facts pursuant to the case
regarding your late husband's sad demise.
Regretfully, a lawsuit has no trace
of merit and therefore we do advise
that evidence a-plenty proves his fall
occurred while in commission of a crime.
No fault accrues to Pig and Pig, et al.
No damages are due you at this time.
His huffing and his puffing further show
a pre-existing illness and although
this wasn't cause of death it surely must
support that bringing suit would be unjust.
Your husband died attempting a break-in
and so this suit is one you cannot win.

From: humptydumpty@wall.com
Subject: Malpractice Claim
To: claimsdesk@fairylandinsurance.net

A horse is not a doctor or a nurse
and so when I came tumbling from that wall
their equine pawing made my breaks much
    worse –
they didn't treat me properly at all.
My x-rays clearly show, as you can see,
how extensively my shell was shattered.
The King's Men also thought they could fix me,
as if, untrained, good thoughts were all that
    mattered.
This failure to provide appropriate care
was thoughtless, mean, immoral and unfair.
I think a million bucks should be enough
to help me past this painful, tragic stuff.
The king's insurance covers this, I'll gamble;
so send the check and smiling, off I'll scramble!

From: jack@cottage.com
Subject: Goose Eggs
To: giant@fefifofum.net

That day I climbed until I reached your house
you roared, I ran, I grabbed your magic bird.
(It honked while I was quiet as a mouse.)
I guess I'm sorry, but you know I heard
you shout you'd grind my bones to make your
        bread!
I'd scaled that beanstalk almost to the sky
but fe-fi-fo-fum scared me, so I fled
in panic that's the only reason why.
My mom and I were hungry and so sad;
I didn't plan to steal. I'm not a bad
boy, just a foolish one. Somehow
I ended up with beans swapped for our cow.
I got the goose and that is how it ends.
Now mom and I are rich. Can't we be friends?

From: giant@fefifofum.net
Subject: re: Goose Eggs
To: jack@cottage.com

You shouldn't have absconded with my goose
when you climbed up that very tall beanstalk.
Eventually I would have turned you loose –
that "grinding bones to bread" was only talk.
Like a thief you broke into my castle
and walked around as if you owned the place.
Surely that entitled me to hassle
you for entering unasked into my space.
I'm sorry that your mom and you were broke
and had to sell your cow to richer folk.
But poverty is no excuse for crime.
You're in grave danger now of doing time.
Return the bird, Jack; all will be forgiven.
Keep it and to prison you'll be driven.

From: hansel@smartkids.org
Subject: Petition For Status As Emancipated Minors
To: dad@woodcutters.net

The time has come. Although I'm still a child
I'll take charge of my life and Gretel's too.
Our documents in court have all been filed
petitioning for rights we feel are due.
Our cruel stepmother said we two kids cost
too much to feed on woodsman's meager pay.
She made you leave us stranded, homeless, lost
in a dark forest on that awful day.
We managed to escape an evil crone
by holding out a scrawny chicken bone.
She was a mean, old, child-devouring witch
but sister Gretel killed the nasty bitch.
Our self-reliance cannot be denied;
parental bonds must now be cast aside.

From: mgooseelementary@fairyland.edu
Subject: Superintendent's Decision
To: mary'smom@cottage.com

Your little daughter caused a huge uproar
with children playing, laughing, acting wild
when her pet lamb came strolling through the
    door.
In short, she is a most unruly child.
The superintendent and the board agree
that her continued presence in the school
can only lead to problems. You must see
that pets in class are quite against the rule.
We know that no child should be left behind
but we must keep the greater good in mind.
Therefore we have decided that it's best
and, most regretfully, we do request
that Mary shall be, for now, suspended
and her lamb's excursions must be ended.

From: goldilocks@momshouse.com
Subject: Property Damage
To: bearx3@cottage.com

Sincerely I regret the damage caused
when I sought refuge in your cozy place.
Tired and lost, I only meant to pause
a moment there then go, leaving no trace.
But I was tempted first by comfy chairs
and then by porridge left behind to cool.
Sleepily I climbed up all the stairs
and napped on baby's bed, I hope that you'll
understand my motives weren't to steal
or vandalize but just to find a meal.
When to my relief, and my delight,
I finally found the things that were just right
I simply thought I'd have a little rest.
I truly didn't mean to be a pest.

From: humanresources@grimmbros.com
Subject: Sexual Harassment Claim
To: gporgie@grimmbros.com

We have received a serious complaint
from fellow-workers sharing office space
alleging that you've failed to show restraint
and acted in a way that's out of place
and violates our handbook rules. You've made
the women cry with each unwanted kiss.
So, Mr. Porgie, it's clear that you've strayed
across the line, and we would be remiss
if we ignored the issues that were raised.
The other men you work with have been
        praised
for comforting those you intimidated.
Serial kissers won't be tolerated.
Sensitivity training is required;
attend the sessions, sir, or you'll be fired!

From: mgoose@fairylaw.com
Subject: Pumpkineater v. Pumpkineater
To: nrimer@mere_l'oye.net

My client in an affidavit swears
that he confined his faithless wife because
she had indulged in numerous affairs –
he didn't think he'd broken any laws.
Her infidelities made him so sad
and left him feeling helpless, in disgrace;
in fact, you might say that she drove him mad
by throwing her *amours* smack in his face.
These acts diminished his capacity
to tell right from wrong. Her audacity
impelled him to this deed. He does regret
his rashness and hopes she can just forget,
forgive and drop the charges that she brought.
He simply was distressed and overwrought.

From: nrimer@mere_l'oye.net
Subject: re: Pumpkineater v. Pumpkineater
To: mgoose@fairylaw.com

Mrs. Pumpkineater's life was hell
when Peter, in a fit of jealous rage,
confined her in a fetid pumpkin shell
no better than a jail cell or a cage.
She swears that she was faithful, always true
and kept her marriage vows although her mate
treated her most harshly in our view.
He threatened violence if she came home late.
She's willing to drop charges and agree
to just divorce the beast, let him go free.
She wishes he would suffer as she did
but asks for nothing more than to be rid
of this abusive, cruel and jealous spouse.
Oh, by the way, she wants the car and house.

From: stepmom@dadsplace.net
Subject: Wedding Wishes
To: cinderella@happilyeverafter.com

Congrats on your betrothal to the Prince –
A joyful day for all of us back here
at home, where we've been celebrating since
we heard the news. I realize, my dear,
perhaps we may have sometimes seemed a bit
harsh in our treatment, but you know we only
meant the best. And now you must admit
it all worked out but, Cindy, we're so lonely!
We miss your smile (although we saw it rarely)
and hope that you won't treat us too unfairly.
I know your sisters took your little shoe
but Charming knew that it belonged to you.
Please, please forgive us. All that's past and
     gone,
so now let's try to make up and move on.

From: mahubbard@cottage.com
Subject: Hubbard v. Bone Thief
To: civilcourt@fairyland.gov

I cannot tell you how distraught I was
when I discovered that I had been robbed.
I stood there speechless, paralyzed because
poor doggie's bones were gone! I sat and sobbed.
Eventually the police caught the thief
but freed him when he had the bones replaced.
Despite my overwhelming shock and grief
all hope for justice was, it seems, misplaced.
The doctor's finding is that I now suffer
a case of PTS that will get tougher
to get past. I want the thief to pay
my costs for therapy and, if I may,
I further ask the court to please assess
damages for my extreme distress.

From: farmer@dell.com
Subject: Termination of Employment
To: lbblue@haystack.net

I've been informed that you again neglected
your duties tending to my cows and sheep.
Instead of keeping the livestock collected
you were discovered hiding, fast asleep.
The sheep were free to wander and to roam
because you failed to ever blow your horn.
It was your job to keep the cow at home;
instead you let her eat up all the corn.
You'll get your final paycheck in a week
less salary for times you chose to sneak
off for a nap beneath that big haystack.
And please don't think I'll ever hire you back!
It surely cannot come as startling news
to learn from this that if you snooze, you lose!

From: neighborhoodassoc@fairyacres.net
Subject: Your Garden
To: marymary@contrary.com

The contents of your garden violate
our Neighborhood Association's rule.
Silverbells and cockleshells are great
but pretty maids all in a row? Not cool!
The concept is quite sexist at the least
objectifying women, so we feel.
A garden gnome or mythologic beast
would be all right. Just something not so real.
You wouldn't put a jockey on your lawn,
so please comply and make your maids be
      gone.
No pink flamingos and no plaster saints –
they're just too tacky; we'd have more
      complaints!
Conventionality is much desired
and here in Fairy Acres it's required.

From: ceo@piperpestprevention.com
Subject: Annoying Kids
To: childwelfare@hamelin.gov

I happily removed the plague of rats
that had made life in Hamelin such a chore,
without the use of poisons or of cats
(exterminators' tools in days of yore).
But then your bratty children came to revel,
following me to village, burg and town.
Their giggling and shrieking would bedevil
the calmest man and cause him to break
        down.
Please retrieve your offspring. Keep them
        home!
They're much too young to wander and
        roam.
And don't think I enticed them to this life.
My time alone was wholly without strife
until this gang of hellions – parasites –
demolished my once-peaceful days and nights.

From: msmuffet@tuffet.net
Subject: Seeking Therapy
To: arachophobesanonymous@fairyclinic.org

My fear of spiders has become a block.
I haven't managed on my own to tough
it out. I've not recovered from the shock
that sent me running, panicked. It's been
        rough!
On top of that, the sight of curds and whey
now causes me to quiver and feel ill.
I used to eat them every single day
but now the very thought gives me a chill.
I was so frightened that I screamed and cried
when that gross spider sat down by my side.
I can't sleep – I should have got beyond it,
learned to just forget the bug that spawned it.
I'm an arachnophobe who cannot cope
I want to join AA. Please give me hope.

From: rumpel.stiltskin@littlecottage.com
Subject: Name Change
To: countyclerk@fairyland.gov

The miller's daughter to my great surprise
has ruined my business plan – a sort of game
that asked contestants to vie for a prize
by guessing my most strange and secret name.
How that was managed she would never tell –
it's not as if I bandied it about.
But she's the queen and my plan's shot to hell.
It looks as if my luck has just run out.
I had ideas – big ones – they're all a bust.
She found me out so I must now adjust.
I've given it much thought and I've assessed
the possibilities that won't be guessed.
Please amend the records; let them show
that my last name is *Stiltskin*, first name *Joe*.

From: districtattorney@fairycourt.gov
Subject: State v. Farmer's Wife
To: grandjury@fairycourt.gov

Regarding claims by Mouse and Mouse and
    Mouse:
details of their de-tailing do support
the charge against the farmer's vicious spouse.
We demand this case be tried in court.
The victims all are visually impaired
and wandered by pure chance across her path.
Under oath they all have so declared,
but she responded with unbridled wrath!
It's clear she meant to take each Mouse's life,
her WMD a carving knife.
We know that rodents often are maligned.
We know society neglects the blind.
The only way the Mice will be requited
is if their assailant is indicted.

From: olwoman@shoe.com
Subject: Need For Larger Home
To: wishingstar@twinkletwinkle.org

This shoe can't hold so many girls and boys;
we simply have to find a larger place.
I've had it up to here with all the noise,
the clutter, the confusion, lack of space.
A home with separate rooms for everyone
would be delightful, and of course a yard
so all the kids can play and have some fun.
There are a lot of us – it might be hard.
You know I can't afford to pay much rent;
I feed and clothe the kids – my money's spent.
I closed my eyes the moment I saw you
wishing you would make my dream come true
that some Samaritan (Bill Gates perhaps?)
would drop some riches in our waiting laps.

From: red@cottage.com
Subject: Gratitude Overdue
To: hunter@forest.net

You looked so handsome in that huntsman
    way
back when I was a frightened little kid
and you came bursting in to save the day.
I never have forgotten what you did.
I was naive, quite fooled when Big Bad lied
that he was Grandmama and so I followed
his request to come close to his side.
Had you not come in then, I'd have been
swallowed!
Back then I had a little girlish crush
that made me stammer, giggle, sigh and blush.
I was a child and gave a childish hug
to you for saving me from that big thug.
But things have changed – now I'm a woman
    grown
and I know lots of ways thanks can be shown.

Marge Hauser's first volume of poetry, Odes of Marge, was published by her mother in a three-ring binder. Since then her work has appeared in Bohemia Art & Literary Journal, Bumbershoot, Cheese It!, First Literary Review – East, Ides of March, The Jewish Women's Literary Annual, The Literary Lawyer, Möbius, The Parkside Poets Collection, Poetica, Point Mass Magazine, Rhyme and PUN-ishment, Tilt-A-Whirl, UltraSounds, and Umbrella,. She is a co-author of Little Perversities (Wasteland Press, 2005). And she is a proud member of the Parkside Poets Collective. When she is not writing poetry she may be found knitting, practicing yoga, or working out with her tai chi broadsword.

Coming soon from NoNet Press:

Flow of Hope, a selection of poetry by
Penelope Maguffin

www.ingramcontent.com/pod-product-compliance
Lightning Source LLC
Chambersburg PA
CBHW060623070426
42449CB00042B/2487